The Complete Guide to
KUNG FU
FIGHTING STYLES

DISCLAIMER

Please note that the publisher of this instructional book is NOT RESPONSIBLE in any manner whatsoever for any injury which may occur by reading and/or following the instructions herein.

It is essential that before following any of the activities, physical or otherwise, herein described, the reader or readers should first consult his or her physician for advice on whether or not the reader or readers should embark on the physical activity described herein. Since the physical activities described herein may be too sophisticated in nature, it is *essential that a physician be consulted.*

UNIQUE PUBLICATIONS

Printed in the United States of America
ISBN: 0-86568-065-5
Library of Congress No.:85-51725

Introduction

Book One: Northern Kung Fu   27

Book Two: Southern Kung Fu   71

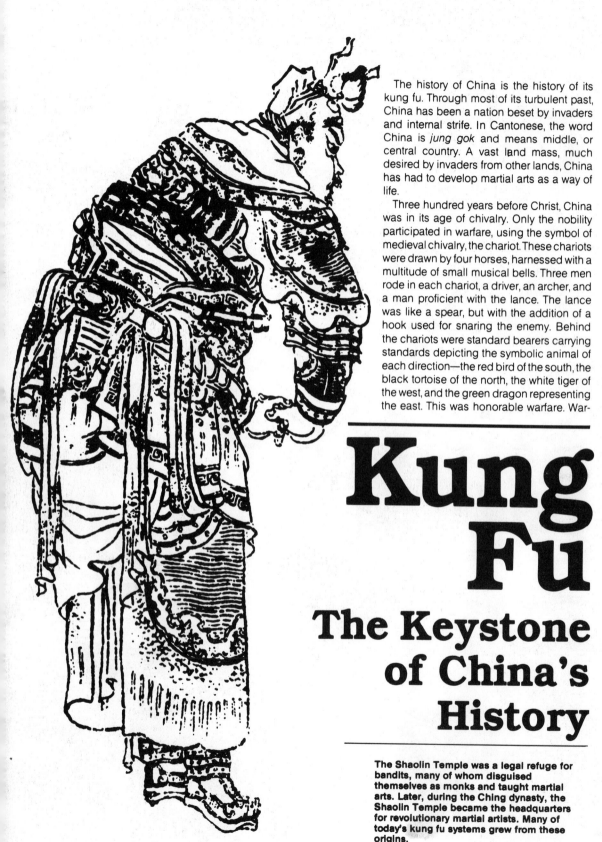

The history of China is the history of its kung fu. Through most of its turbulent past, China has been a nation beset by invaders and internal strife. In Cantonese, the word China is *jung gok* and means middle, or central country. A vast land mass, much desired by invaders from other lands, China has had to develop martial arts as a way of life.

Three hundred years before Christ, China was in its age of chivalry. Only the nobility participated in warfare, using the symbol of medieval chivalry, the chariot. These chariots were drawn by four horses, harnessed with a multitude of small musical bells. Three men rode in each chariot, a driver, an archer, and a man proficient with the lance. The lance was like a spear, but with the addition of a hook used for snaring the enemy. Behind the chariots were standard bearers carrying standards depicting the symbolic animal of each direction—the red bird of the south, the black tortoise of the north, the white tiger of the west, and the green dragon representing the east. This was honorable warfare. War-

Kung Fu

The Keystone of China's History

The Shaolin Temple was a legal refuge for bandits, many of whom disguised themselves as monks and taught martial arts. Later, during the Ching dynasty, the Shaolin Temple became the headquarters for revolutionary martial artists. Many of today's kung fu systems grew from these origins.

riors from opposing armies would often drink together before a battle.

Then came the period of the "Warring States" (300 B.C.). During the era, chivalry gave way to warfare carried on by adventurers or knight-errants. They were literally soldiers-of-fortune. The chariot was replaced by mounted archers, cavalry, and an abundance of foot soldiers. Many of the lone adventurers became famous as escorts for the nobility and rich traveling through the countryside. Because there was violence everywhere, these escorts had to be good fighters. Martial arts among the civilian population of China began to gain importance.

In 246 B.C., the first emperor of the Ch'in dynasty came to power. He assumed the name, Ch'in Shih-huang-ti, or "first emperor of the Ch'in." Known to history as the "Chinese Caesar," Shih-huang-ti was able to do what none before had accomplished, unite China into a complete empire. He ruled China with an iron hand, enslaving multitudes to build the Great Wall of China, and burning all books which might conflict with his rigid rule. He also prohibited the practice of martial arts and the carrying of weapons by civilians.

From Mercenary to Emperor

It was the next emperor, an adventurer named Liu Pang, who turned China back to the study of martial arts. He was originally an escort, a freelance martial artist. One day while escorting a band of prisoners to jail, Liu Pang decided to free them and become their leader. He led his rapidly growing army of ruffians throughout China and soon assumed the throne, from soldier-of-fortune to emperor. Liu Pang became the first emperor of the Han dynasty, destined to rule China for four centuries (202 B.C.—220 A.D.).

It was Liu Pang who said, "It was while dressed in rough cloth and wielding a three-foot sword that I conquered the empire!" He was truly a soldier's king, and from his influence, martial arts flourished throughout the Han dynasty.

During the era of the Han dynasty, a physician named Hua-to originated a series of exercises depicting animal movements, which were called the "five animals play." They were designed to strengthen the body, both externally and internally, and represented the tiger, deer, monkey, bird, and bear. Although not originally meant to be used as martial arts, Hua-to's five animal exercises are thought by many to be the forerunners of kung fu animal forms.

It is said that the Buddhist monk Bodhiddharma brought martial arts, along with Buddhism, to China from India, and that the center of this Buddhist martial art was the Shaolin temple of northern china. Historians who think that Bodhidharma brought kung fu to China are wrong. China had kung fu long before Bodhidharma came. He did bring Buddhism to China, along with a series of exercises to keep the monks physically fit between their long periods of meditation and inactivity.

Buddhism is a non-violent religion, so it seems unlikely that the monks would allow the practice of fighting within their temples and monasteries. However, the temples were legal refuges where men hunted by the law could find sanctuary. Many of these desperate men were excellent fighters and, while disguised as monks, taught their martial arts to other fighters.

Revolutionary Fighters

This sort of sanctuary and protection from government forces reached a peak during the Ching dynasty (A.D. 1644-1911), when revolutionary martial artists were engaged in rebellious activities while headquartered in the safety of the Shaolin temple. Kung fu systems like choy-li-fut, hung gar, and white eyebrow grew from such origins.

In retaliation, the Manchurian government of the Ching dynasty burned the Shaolin temple, forcing the rebels to go into hiding and to form secret societies, such as the Triad and White Lotus societies.

Secret societies became focal points for anti-foreign sentiments during the Boxer Rebellion, at the end of the 19th century. Unfortunately, the Boxers, who had been trained to believe that they were invulnerable to injury from any weapons, found that they were no match for the bullets of the Westerner's firearms.

Martial arts spread throughout China during the Republic (A.D. 1912-1948). Military tactics were taught in all schools, and fighting arts became very popular in China.

When the Communists took over China in 1948, the study of kung fu ceased completely. Many martial arts teachers escaped to Hong Kong and Taiwan to continue teaching kung fu. Several years ago, kung fu returned to Mainland China in the form of wushu. Wushu is an acrobatic martial art that, until very recently, has been lacking in the fighting essence that characterizes Chinese kung fu. However, with the popularity of kung fu throughout the world, China has started incorporating more and more traditional kung fu into wushu forms, thus returning it to a fighting art.

Hong Kong is at the southern tip of China. Therefore, many of the kung fu systems, hung gar, wing chun, and choy-li-fut, for instance, have origins in southern China. And Taiwan, which had a predominance of Chinese immigrants from Northern China, contains many of the northern styles (chang chuan, pa kwa, northern praying mantis).

Kung Fu Comes to America

Until the early 1960s, kung fu in the United States was seldom taught to non-Chinese. Many of the Chinese immigrants were virtually confined to the Chinatowns of their cities. There existed a certain amount of racial prejudice between the Americans of that time and the Chinese not born in this country. Chinese were looked upon as second-class citizens, immigrants from a poor impoverished country, here to take advantage of America's wealth. This, coupled with the fact that most Americans are bigger and taller than the average Chinese, led Chinese kung fu sifus to refuse to teach any non-Chinese. After all, why teach a fighting art to someone bigger that he, who might turn around and use that knowledge against him? Kung fu was the only self-defense that most Chinese had.

Those Americans who desired kung fu training at that time often received what education they could get from students of Chinese sifus, students who were sometimes only at a beginner's level. Since these students-turned-instructors were not qualified teachers, their American students many times learned only dance-like forms devoid of power or application. Kung fu got the reputation of containing only soft artistic movements, instead of practical self-defense techniques.

Bruce and the Bomb

In 1964, Mainland China tested an atomic bomb and Bruce Lee debuted in the *Green Hornet* television series, two events that awakened Americans to China and its martial arts. China had been thought of as a poor underdeveloped country, but now emerged as a world power. Americans found a new interest in Chinese culture, including the arts, language, food, and martial arts. As Bruce Lee continued his movie career as a kung fu hero, American audiences hungered to learn the fighting arts of China.

Along with this new cultural thirst, came

18

more respect for the Chinese people and their traditions. Previous hard relations between Chinese and Americans softened immensely. Many Chinese sifus (teachers) started to teach their martial arts to non-Chinese students. The great interest by Americans in learning Chinese culture and martial arts encouraged many highly-rated kung fu sifus to immigrate from Hong Kong and Taiwan to the United States, to teach the American public.

This does not necessarily mean that to be a good kung fu instructor, one must be Chinese. Because kung fu is relatively new to the United States, many of the good teachers are Chinese, but just as there are well qualified non-Chinese kung fu sifus, there are also some Chinese instructors who don't have the proper background and experience to teach martial arts.

A good kung fu teacher should have received his training from a qualified master, who in turn had a thorough background in Chinese martial arts. Of course, it depends on what the student himself wants. If he wishes to learn the basics of a system and no more, and there is an instructor in his area who knows and teaches only the basics, then that may suit his needs. However, if the student wants to progress to a higher level of training, then he should seek the teacher that has attained that level himself.

Searching for a Sifu

Here is a basic outline for locating the right teacher:

1) Check the background of the sifu's teachers. How close to the founder of the system is he? Someone who is of the third generation usually has a stronger and more traditional foundation in that style than a sifu who is ten generations removed. Of course, the age of the kung fu system should also be considered. It's impossible to be of the third generation in a style 300 years old.

2) How long has the sifu been teaching? Experience usually improves anyone's teaching qualities.

3) How good are his advanced students? As a rule, the advanced students of a good instructor will be able to duplicate the sifu's ability by at least 60 percent.

4) How traditional is the sifu? Where are his roots? The art is developed by individuals, but past knowledge of a system is important for a foundation.

5) What is the student looking for, better form, self-defense, tournament competition?

Preceding page: Sifu Brendan Lai thrills a crowd with a demonstration of praying mantis. Below and right: As Kwai Chang Caine, a half-breed Shaolin monk, David Carradine helped make "kung fu" a household word thanks to the popularity of the series *Kung Fu*.

Does the sifu teach what the individual student is looking for?

Some responsibility for determining the teachers' qualities lies on the student himself. The kung fu student should not expect to learn everything there is to know immediately. All good and lasting information and techniques take time to learn. The amount of material that a sifu does teach to each individual student depends upon the student's sincerity, effort, and desire. And the fact remains that most kung fu sifus who have something of value to teach reserve it for those few students who show the above qualities. So a student should not expect to learn the "secrets" of a kung fu system until he has proven himself deserving of that knowledge.

A good instructor is not fussy or picky. He should initially make his martial art simple and easy to learn. After the student learns and understands the movements, then a good sifu will take the time to correct his student on the fine points. If the sifu is too much of a perfectionist, he will discourage many of his students, especially those without any martial arts background.

A qualified kung fu instructor will always teach his students the application and theory behind each technique. He will provide a complete and correct training program, and share his knowledge to the limits of the student's interest and ability.

It's a fallacy that some kung fu systems are limited to certain sizes and types of people. Each style contains separate forms and training procedures to fit all sizes, shapes, and interests of students. Even those styles that are supposed to be only external or internal have much in common.

In their advanced forms, so-called external or internal systems all become the same, a mixture of both hard and soft. Even tai chi chuan, reputed to be only a soft internal system, contains a blend of hard external powers along with the soft in its advanced level of training. The only difference is that external styles (choy-li-fut, hung gar) start with hard power and then progress to internal strengths in higher stages of training, while the internal systems (tai chi, hsing-i), start out soft and internal and add hard power in the advanced levels of training.

Top: Once a kung fu master in Mainland China, Chan Poi now teaches authentic wah lum praying mantis to his American students. Here he practices splits on the *mook yum jong* poles. Above: Sifu Y.C. Wong is a highly learned and respected sifu who teaches hung gar, a Southern system, in San Francisco, California.

Northern Kung Fu: Opening the Door

A Chinese saying about Northern kung fu systems, loosely translated, states: "Two hands are like two doors, and it takes footwork to open those doors." In other words, the opponent's hands can close most avenues of attack, but good footwork can penetrate or "open" these doors, allowing access to the opponent.

Kung fu of Northern China traditionally relies on active footwork, moving in all directions, to penetrate or break through an opponent's defenses. In Southern China, footwork is not as active. The Southerners use their hands, called "iron bridge," and a strong solid stance to repel oncoming attacks.

As a rule, Northern systems teach soft movements and soft power first, slowly advancing to harder more external techniques, and ending with a necessary mixture of both hard and soft. In the South, where many systems developed from a need for quickly-learned revolutionary fighting tactics, hard is learned first. Soft internal strength is the next stage, and the end result is the same as with the Northern styles, a blending of hard and soft.

The following pages provide an introduction to chang chuan, Northern praying mantis, monkey style, eagle claw, hsing-i, pa kwa, and tai chi chuan. These arts are among the most popular and most effective of the Northern systems.

長拳

Chang Chuan
The Brave Father of Chinese Kung Fu

Perhaps the original kung fu system, chang chuan's powerful, courageous, and free-spirited techniques have made it one of the most important styles in both China and America.

Much has been said about the origins of karate, tae kwon do, judo, etc., but nobody is certain about the beginnings of kung fu, as we know it today. Of course, there's the Shaolin temple story—however, that is fairly recent history. The Chinese have been using the martial arts for thousands of years, both among themselves and against others, but organized kung fu needed a father system from which to evolve. Recorded history is sparse on the subject. However, there are many indications that kung fu originated from the *chang chuan* (long fist) system.

Chang chuan is reported to have been created during the reign of Tai Tzu, the first emperor of the Sung dynasty (AD 960-976).

A picturesque, wide-open style of kung-fu, chang chuan is characterized by the courageous, bold, and free spirit of the Sung dynasty. It rapidly gained popularity with the farmers of Northern China, who, after working hard all year to harvest their crops, needed something physical to practice to keep fit during the long winter months.

Martial arts teachers would set up schools in several villages and travel between them,

teaching their art until the villagers either grew tired of them, or another kung fu master showed up to challenge and take over if he won.

The kung fu systems in rural China became very mixed, because so many masters taught the same system, but with varying degrees of expertise. A typical village might have five or six martial arts teachers within a three year period, all teaching their version of chang chuan kung fu. This was how a popular system spread, and also how it could become very mixed and different from village to village. From that blending, came variations of chang chuan, such as Northern Shaolin (Sil Lum in Cantonese). Northern Shaolin, although not pure chang chuan, is close enough to be easily mistaken for it. Northern Shaolin is actually a form of chang chuan that was enlarged upon during the last part of the Ming and the first part of the Ching dynasties, hence the name Shaolin, which is misleading since it suggests Buddhist origins.

In more modern history, the chang chuan system was the predominant style of kung fu during the Chinese Republic, and at the same time became popular in Shanghai and Nanking; then, during the second world war, spread to Canton and Hong Kong, where it is seen integrated into many other styles, both Southern and Northern, such as choy-li-fut and Northern praying mantis.

A Bold and Honest Style

Chang means a wide open or long movement and *chuan* means fist, hence "long fist." The system is open, not a closed hidden-away style like some short-hand kung fu styles. It's a brave honest system containing many beautiful straightforward movements. Chang chuan is a symbol of a brave, bold China where the fighters had the attitude that the best man will win, without any tricks or deception. It's a valuable system from which to learn the basics of kung fu, since the footwork and stances are extremely strong and balanced. Chang chuan isn't a specialized system, and includes many different hand and foot techniques. Because of this, the founders of many other kung fu systems chose to draw from chang chuan to improve and enrich their own budding styles. Systems such as six-harmony praying mantis, lo han, mi-sung, hung gar, and choy-li-fut contain a significant amount of the chang chuan system.

One important feature of chang chuan, that others have adopted, is its honesty and spirit. The attitude that the bravest and boldest will win always inspires confidence in the martial artist. Wushu, the fast moving acrobatic martial art of Mainland China, uses chang chuan predominately because of that same bold attitude. The wushu performer has a tremendous amount of spirit, due mostly to the influence of chang chuan.

The chang chuan system is seen extensively throughout Chinese opera. Chinese opera adopted the chang chuan style, partly because of its growing popularity as a martial art and partly because of its spirited style. The art's graceful and acrobatic forms mixed easily with the opera movements.

The North Kicks

Chang chuan is characterized by wide open sweeping arm and fist movements, low stances, and high kicks. Those same high kicks are one of the reasons for the old Chinese axiom, "the North kicks, the South

---

Chang chuan is a symbol of a brave, bold China where the fighters had the attitude that the best man will win . . . without any tricks or deception.

---

punches." People have a mistaken idea that since chang chuan is a prominent Northern style and has an abundance of high kicks, that high kicks are indicative of Northern China's kung fu. The high kicks are actually for practice, not for fighting. The actual kicks used in combat are low, below the waist, and the many high kicks and jump kicks are for training purposes only.

Chang chuan is an excellent exercise to promote good health. The system encourages strong stances, straight backs, and relaxed supple waists and shoulders. An open, upright style, its practitioners derive much of their strength from their courage. The soft internal art of tai chi chuan took many of its postures from chang chuan.

Chang chuan isn't specialized like other kung fu systems such as wing chun or white eyebrow *(bak mei)*. The art has many different forms to learn, and there is no special order in which to learn these forms, unlike Northern praying mantis, which has a structured numerical order to teach the sets.

Chang chuan provides the strongest foundation for learning weapons: since the system is generalized, it includes almost all Chinese weapons. The weapons forms are like the hand forms, open, circular, and beautiful to watch. With its beautiful movements, chang chuan has become a very popular style in the forms competition of American martial arts tournaments.

Jason Tsou shows the wide open, sweeping arm movements that are characteristic of chang chuan, "long fist,"—the father of many kung fu styles.

An open and brave system, chang chuan is a valuable style which teaches the basics of kung fu, since stances and footwork are strong and balanced—which is why other, more recent systems have drawn on its techniques.

Despite Northern systems being characterized as "kicking" styles, chang chuan offers great versatility, combining low, long, stable stances with sweeping hand techniques, making it a favorite with Chinese opera stars.

北方螳螂

Northern Praying Mantis
The Power of the Claw

Combining the incredible arm and hand strength of the praying mantis with the quick footwork of the monkey creates this mercilessly effective self-defense system.

The praying mantis insect, with his blinding speed and incredible strength in his front legs and scissor-like claws, is personified in Chinese kung fu through the *tong lun* or praying mantis system. Like the insect after which it is patterned, praying mantis is a ferocious self-defense system, a style that gives its opponents no mercy. The mantis practitioner will typically block a punch, grab with his blocking hand and pull his attacker off-balance, then close into him while simultaneously striking with the opposite hand. He may counter his opponent's attack with three to five lightning quick movements, using the theory that "once you hit with the first, your opponent's guard is down, and you follow with three or four more strikes to totally disable him."

Praying mantis originated toward the end of the Ming dynasty. Prior to the Ming dynasty,

Chinese martial arts were on a downward trend, possibly due to the prohibitive influence of Mongol invaders. The Ming dynasty became a period of rebuilding for kung fu in China. Martial arts had become vague and dance-like. So kung fu masters studied many different systems and blended them together in order to improve their martial arts and increase their practicality for fighting. Praying mantis was a result of this period of rebuilding.

According to tradition, praying mantis originated in the East Shan-Tung province of China. Its founder was a master of a very high level in kung fu named Wong Long. Wong Long studied the insect's fighting techniques, and from them, developed the trademark of praying mantis: the mantis claw *(gou)*, a grabbing motion that derives all of its power from the wrist and forearm. Wong

Long also observed the manner in which monkeys move and from that created the mantis "monkey step," a quick and balanced method of footwork. When attacked, the mantis practitioner can move easily in any direction with amazing speed and balance.

The mantis style that Wong Long founded is called "seven-star praying mantis." In Chinese martial arts, seven-star means "always moving and changing your direction, in order to break down your opponent's guard."

Mantis Hand Moves

Instead of using either straight or circular movements, praying mantis uses both equally. There are four distinctive hand movements of seven-star praying mantis.

1) The mantis claw, or gou, is a sideways and outside block and grab with emphasis on the last three fingers of the hand, which combined with the forearm muscle form a vise-like grip on the mantis' opponent. The back of the hand (called a negative gou) is often used to strike with. In this position, the mantis might strike up into his opponent's chin, throat or armpit. The gou is neither hard nor soft, but is a 50-50 combination of the two, using only the hand and forearm for power and strength.

2) *Lau* is a circular motion from the outside toward the inside, using the palm to strike with, usually a downward movement.

3) The third is *tsai,* a forward motion that may be followed by a grab using all of the fingers of the hand.

4) *Qua* is the fourth basic hand technique of praying mantis. This is an upward and backward movement of the arm to block an oncoming blow.

The mantis practitioner can move in four directions with his four basic hand techniques, and he rapidly changes from one move to another, forming many different combinations with which to confuse his attacker.

The footwork of seven-star praying mantis includes such movements as *san,* an elusive fast movement to the side of the oncoming

Left: Sifu Brendan Lai strikes a deep seven star praying mantis stance while flourishing a single broadsword. Right: Lai strikes to one of the mantis man's favorite targets: the throat.

attacker; *tsun,* to turn away from the attacker's blow; *ton,* the praying mantis hop; *non,* to change position and gain advantage.

Wong Long created seven-star praying mantis with the intention of having a very clear, quickly learned, but powerful fighting system.

Toward the end of the Ching dynasty and

Like the insect after which it is patterned, praying mantis is a ferocious self-defense system, a style that gives its opponents no mercy.

---

the beginning of the Republic, a very knowledgeable praying mantis master appeared. Chun Hua Lung had mastered the seven-star mantis system, and wished to place more emphasis on footwork to bring the mantis practitioner in closer to his opponent. Chun had friends who were masters of hsing-i, which is straightforward and powerful, and of tom bei, a soft and circular martial art. He combined some of the hsing-i and tom bei movements with seven-star praying mantis, with the emphasis on moving footwork—not just stances, and from that developed the "eight-steps" praying mantis style.

Chun coordinated the hands and footwork together as one and brought the mantis fighter in much closer to his opponent then does the seven-star style. Eight-steps uses the same original mantis hands, *gou, lau, tsai,* and *qua,* but differs in the footwork. The footwork of eight-steps praying mantis consists of moving in so close to the enemy that he doesn't have room to move and counterattack. The eight-steps practitioner is almost sticking to his opponent, and has "closed the door" to all retaliation.

Internal Power

There are those who wish to add more meaning and depth to every martial art. A praying mantis master, Wei San, found that opportunity when he created "six-harmony" praying mantis. An offshoot of seven-star, six-harmony was developed to add more internal power to the art. The basic principle of the six-harmony style is that the six body functions—eyes, hands, body, spirit, *chi* (internal energy), and soul—should interact together

in harmony. Again, six-harmony praying mantis uses the four basic mantis hands. However, after the four basic hands, six-harmony differs greatly. The six-harmony praying mantis sticks to and feels his opponent's next move, much the same as in tai chi chuan fighting techniques. The opponent has no move to make, because the mantis is instinctively aware of even the most subtle move.

The "tai chi praying mantis" is an even more recent development. Tai mantis practitioners are unique because they use in their fighting what is called the "trading off" theory of praying mantis. Ferocious fighters, the tai mantis actually lets his opponent's punch strike him, or may deflect it slightly by quickly twisting his body to the side. In return, he is in very close to his opponent and can strike back with a much more powerful blow, usually dead center to the opponent. This technique is reserved for serious fighting only, since if the praying mantis misjudges a little bit, he can be seriously injured or can injure his opponent with his powerful close-in strike.

Tai mantis practitioners train by toughening the arms, legs, and body by hitting themselves repeatedly with hard objects, and by two-man contact sparring. It is often said that, "If you spar with a tai chi mantis, every time you hit him, you're helping him train."

Some kung fu systems rely on distinguishing characteristics to make them unique, such as special hands, sticking techniques, special footwork, or different ways to convey power and deliver the punch. But praying mantis is unique, in that it combines these special techniques into one system, and uses them all with equal importance.

From Rams to Mice

Praying mantis has fighting styles that apply to everyone. For the large person who has a lot of power, but isn't quite as quick and agile as a smaller person, there are ramming techniques. Ramming uses the mantis practitioner's size and weight, combined with speed, to blitz the opponent with either punches or open hand pushes.

The smaller praying mantis student has at his disposal a method of fighting called "mouse running around." That style requires a quick, agile person with a very flexible waist, as he will be ducking, jumping, and darting in and out much the same as a mouse.

The student of praying mantis with a medium build who has some speed and more power than the small person, can use jumping, flipping, and ramming techniques to his advantage. The praying mantis system is versatile enough to allow its students to specialize in whatever type of technique that fits them best and still have a large arsenal of moves to use to their own advantage.

Left: Sifu Paul Eng of Palo Alto, California here demonstrates the mantis claw and the deadly footwork of the monkey, a beautiful yet lethal combination.

Monkey Style
From Man into Monkey

The martial artist must virtually become a monkey—with all of the simian's trickery and acrobatic skills— to master this versatile art.

Monkey kung fu, famous throughout Northern China for its tumbling and rolling techniques, the confusing and constantly changing footwork, and its deadly accuracy, was founded by a martial artist with a short temper. As the legends have it, that same short temper put Kao Tze behind bars in ancient China for killing a fellow villager in a fight. The prison had two exit gates: the first guarded by a group of chattering monkeys and the second by human jailers. Kao Tze observed that any prisoner attempting an escape had to get through the gate guarded by the monkeys first. Not only was no one successful at this venture, but the monkeys were fierce fighters and in each case severely injured the escapees.

So impressed was Kao Tze that he carefully studied the monkeys at play and while fighting. He noticed that each primate had his own style of fighting, which made it impossible for the escaping prisoner to defend against the monkeys' onslaught. Kao Tze broke these separate styles down into five basic monkey fighting patterns.

When his prison term ended and he had returned to freedom, Kao Tze set about devising the *tai sing* or monkey style kung fu system.

One of Kao Tze's most renown students was Gung Da Hoi, who combined tai sing kung fu with the pap kar kung fu system and founded the tai sing pap kar moon system. Gung Da Hoi was the sifu of Chan Sau Chung of Hong Kong, the world famous Monkey King. Chan Sau Chung is known throughout the world for his monkey kung fu.

Five Types of Monkeys

Tai sing pap kar moon is broken down into the five original monkey types. There is a form among these five that will fit any monkey practitioner.

1) The first is the "drunken monkey." Mon-

keys become easily intoxicated when they drink. When the monkey appears to be drunk, his enemies attack, thinking to take advantage of his condition. But the monkey is very elusive and hard to catch. He hides, then counterattacks with deadly precision. His footwork consists of low stances and tricky acrobatics, giving the appearance of drunkeness.

The drunken monkey is the hardest of the five types to learn, but it is the most powerful of the five. In this form, the monkey must squat, roll, and tumble more than in the others. The movements are combinations of hard and soft power, designed to develop the *chi* or internal energy. Although the monkey seems unstable and out of control, when he moves he concentrates his energy into whatever part of his body he wishes. This can be the monkey practitioner's shoulder, waist, hip, arms, etc.. Wherever he touches his opponent, the chi energy leaves the mon-

The monkey must be sly and tricky ... he must be devilish and unpredictable.

key's body and can cause serious injury to his opposition. Everything seems relaxed, without hard external power, but upon contact, powerful internal energy is released.

2) The "stone monkey" uses more physical force than the drunken monkey and is a much more external form. The stone monkey is well suited to a physically strong person. All of the movements use force against force. This monkey practitioner trains his body to be very resilient to blows, like a rock. He can exchange punches on a one-to-one basis without feeling his opponent's blows. This form also contains many falling and rolling techniques.

3) The "lost monkey" has lost his way, and looks innocent and confused. This is just a fraud, for the lost monkey is tricky, and deceiving, fooling his opponent at every opportunity. This monkey trains for extremely light footwork. He's quick to move, and each movement (both fist and foot) is hard for the opposition to predict and follow. Sometimes

Left: Wushu performer Wang Ju performs on the monkey staff. Right: Chan San Chung, a Hong Kong master of monkey style, assumes a low and close-in stance. The raised leg, braced by the left hand, can attack in a low kick, while the poised right hand can lash out in a strike.

he seems to fake a move, but then it turns out to be real, and vice versa.

The lost monkey changes his footwork frequently. His opposition doesn't know where the monkey is moving next. The same is true for his hands. The hands and footwork change suddenly and without warning.

4) The "standing monkey" doesn't fall and roll as much as the others, and uses more conventional stances. It is a long-arm form which is well suited for tall people.

5) The "wooden monkey" is a very aggressive fighter. He is relentless in his attack, and nevers fears his opponent. The wooden monkey uses quiet, controlled movements. He's always looking for an opening in his opponent's defenses. When he attacks, he attacks so aggressively that his enemy finds it practically impossible to defend himself. This monkey is the opposite of the playful-appearing drunken monkey.

There are five principles describing the monkey personality that are the essence of monkey fighting.

1) He must be sly and tricky.

2) He must be poison to his adversary, like a poisonous snake.

3) He must be able to destroy the opponent's attack.

4) He must be good at bluffing his adversary.

5) He must be devilish and unpredictable, like a monkey.

The student of monkey kung fu incorporates these five principles into his own personality while performing or fighting.

Monkey Training

The first form learned in the tai sing system is the basic training set. This form is called *day tong sai ping kuen* or "ground four level fist." It concentrates on ground techniques such as rolling and falling. This form is taught first to develop the student's body, so that he won't be hurt when he tumbles and falls. The monkey student always learns this set before any of the five monkey forms.

Next, the students learn the monkey footwork, with the aid of a device called *jou sing* or "running rope." The monkey student holds tightly to a suspended rope and practices monkey footwork, while supporting the top half of his body with his grip on the rope. This way, he learns to move quickly and lightly.

After that, the monkey students learn the monkey fist techniques. The monkey uses all parts of his body to strike with: fist, claw hand, elbow, knee, foot and monkey paw.

The only weapon in the monkey system is the monkey staff or *tai sing moon* staff. This is a very acrobatic staff form, comprised of many jumping, tumbling, and rolling techniques.

Monkey kung fu is a system based on animal movements that goes beyond just imitating the animal's footwork or fighting movements. The monkey's attitude is an important part of the system's success as a fighting style. Therefore, unlike praying mantis or white crane, the monkey practitioner must think and act like a monkey before he can be successful at his martial art.

Paulie Zink, a skilled monkey stylist, demonstrates the low twisted stances and extreme flexibility required by his art. Right: Chan San Fung's skill is so great that he is often called the "monkey king" of Hong Kong.

Eagle Claw
108 Points of Attack

With the ability to attack any of the body's 108 pressure points with his powerful talons, the eagle claw practitioner can totally control and immobilize his assailant.

The fierce eagle uses his sharp talons to ensnare his prey. When the victim is trapped within his vise-like grip, the powerful bird quickly dispatches it. The eagle uses a combination of cleverness, speed, and strength to trap and hold his prey. This is the same combination that eagle claw kung fu uses to fight and defend with.

Eagle claw (ying jao in Cantonese) is a very old system, founded 850 years ago by a Chinese general, Ouk Fay. Fashioned after the fierce fighting bird, eagle claw didn't become popular with the Chinese kung fu practitioners until the turn of the 20th century.

At first glance, eagle claw looks like jujitsu. There are an abundance of joint locks and quick takedowns. There are no unnecessary movements, and every move is performed at full speed. The purpose of eagle claw is not to kill or maim, but to catch and control the enemy, so speed is an essential factor.

The complete eagle claw system is divided into 108 striking points, of which 36 are secret *dim muc* (lethal) pressure point strikes. The other 72 are also pressure point attacks, but aren't killing or crippling strikes. The human body contains pressure points, similar to acupuncture points, which mark sensitive and vital areas, areas which control pain, movement, and even life itself.

Claw Hand Technique

The initial phase of eagle claw kung fu is the claw hand technique. The eagle practitioner uses his claw hand to stop his opponent's attack and to immobilize his opposition. With his eagle claw, he controls the adversary's arms, joints, and muscles. He can stop an attack, inflict pain at a sensitive pressure point, or use the claw hand for a

jujitsu-like joint lock. The eagle practitioner effectively uses his eagle claw on all parts of the opponent's body.

The claw hand is made by folding all of the fingers of the hand into a half-clenched position. From this position, the eagle practitioner can use his fingers to grab, pull, or twist the opposition into submission. He can even temporarily paralyze his enemy with the claw hand.

Speed is an important factor in eagle claw. Eagle claw students train for speed and accuracy by grabbing pieces of material and feathers whipping through the air. They strengthen their fingers by catching tree branches that are snapped back toward them.

All blows are made to the sensitive pressure points of the body. Eagle claw students study acupuncture charts to learn and memorize the exact location of these pressure points. In ancient China, before acupuncture became popular, eagle practitioners used only the tips of their fingers to deliver a blow. They would strike anywhere on their opponent's body. Because the striking area of the

"The system is not hard to learn, but is very dangerous . . ."

fingertips was very small, all of their energy was concentrated, doing more damage. Needless to say, they strengthened and conditioned their fingertips rigorously to withstand the force of their own blows.

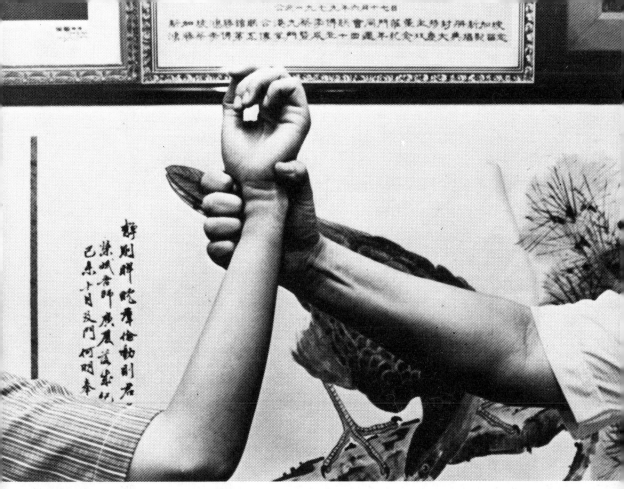

Left: Shum Leung of
New York City shows
how the eagle claw
grip at the neck and
wrist, combined with
a simple foot sweep,
can disable an
enemy. Above: The
eagle claw grasps
and then controls an
opponent's attacking
limb. Overleaf: Gini
Lau, daughter of
famed eagle claw
master Lau Fat
Mang, immobilizes
the wrist of her
opponent while
breaking his arm.

In present times, with the knowledge of acupuncture available, the eagle practitioner still uses his fingers to strike, but also knows instantly which part of his opponent's body is most susceptible to his blow.

Painful Joint Locks

The eagle stylist uses every imaginable joint lock and takedown. Not only are they experts at pressure point attacks, but they know how to use painful joint locks, with a maximum of speed and a minimum of wasted energy. Even the eagle claw kicks are directed toward controlling and subduing the opposition. Many of the kicks are actually locking techniques, using the foot to trap the other person. Rather than using leg sweeps, some of the eagle claw kicks become rolling leg locks that bring the adversary into the striking range of the eagle claw stylist.

When the different phases of the eagle claw system are put together, the claw hand is used initially to block and trap the opposition's blow, and to pull and keep him within range; the joint-locking techniques further immobilize him; and the pressure point strikes completely remove him from the fighting arena.

The eagle claw system is suited perfectly for a variety of different applications. For instance, it is a good self-defense style for women. Since eagle claw doesn't advocate

the use of force against force, but instead places the emphasis on control, women find it easy to use.

Eagle claw is also useful for any police work that involves disarming and disabling a suspected felon. The joint locks and pressure point attacks are perfect for this kind of police work.

Eagle claw stances are similar to other systems such as Northern Shaolin or choy-li-fut. Eagle is basically a long arm style which employs long reaching grabs and very circular joint locks. The main difference between eagle claw and other systems is that it is never used to kill or maim—only to catch and temporarily disable the opponent.

There are 10 essential forms in the eagle claw system. All are empty-hand sets. There are no weapon sets in eagle claw. Within these 10 hand forms are contained 108 different eagle claw techniques, just as there are 108 different pressure point strikes. Each claw hand technique is a necessary part of the system.

Sifu Cheh Wing Bun of Hong Kong, a famous eagle claw master, explains that only a few students can be taught eagle claw kung fu because, "The system is not hard to learn, but is very dangerous and can be used to kill or seriously hurt someone." This is one reason that eagle claw is not taught extensively throughout the kung fu community.

形
意

Hsing-I
The No-Nonsense Art

The simple, straightforward techniques of hsing-i can lead the advanced practitioner to mastery of internal power.

Based on the premise that fighting should be ended as quickly as it is started, hsing-i practitioners use simple direct techniques to overcome their adversaries. And yet, coupled with this no-nonsense practical ideology is one of the highest levels of internal kung fu systems.

Hsing-i is an old system, originating near the beginning of the Ching dynasty (about 1640 AD). It was founded by Chi Chi-ki, a martial artist from Shansi province.

The name hsing-i can be translated as "shape of mind" or "shape of intention," a definition which applies whether the hsing-i being practiced is the more commonly seen external form of straightforward fighting or the highest level of hsing-i, which utilizes the practitioner's chi to perform incredible feats.

There are three schools or styles of hsing-i. The first and original school is the Shansi style. It was the style of the founder, Chi Chi-ki. The Shansi school branched out to form the Hopei style and Honan style founded by Li Neng-jang and Ma Hsueh-li respectively. These three schools are very different forms of hsing-i. The original Shansi style is seldom seen today. It is concerned mostly with soft internal strengths and there are few teachers available in present times with the extensive background necessary to teach that form of hsing-i.

The Hopei style (named for the province where it prevailed) is now the most common form of hsing-i taught. It is easy for beginners and the student can be successful at it without having to delve deeply into hsing-i's internal aspects.

Five Elements—Twelve Animals

A major part of the hsing-i system is comprised of forms depicting the Chinese five elements (earth, metal, water, wood, and fire)

and twelve animal forms (dragon, tiger, monkey, horse, chicken, falcon, snake, tai bird, lizard, swallow, eagle, and bear).

The five elements each correspond to a

The most advanced level of hsing-i deals with the delivery of hua chin, where the hsing-i stylist emits power without apparent physical force.

certain portion of the human body. They also represent five types of fighting power. The five element fists form the basic training of hsing-i.

The 12 animals give hsing-i flavor and variety. Besides imitating the animal's movements, hsing-i incorporates the spirit of each animal into its techniques. For instance, the tiger becomes quick and powerful, the monkey is agile and tricky, and the dragon is strong and ferocious. Through the 12 animal forms, the hsing-i practitioner begins to train his internal energy to respond to conscious thought.

Hsing-i uses direct linear strikes combined with secure practical footwork. There are three hand techniques in hsing-i. They are the regular closed fist practiced by beginners; the phoenix eye fist employed by more advanced practitioners; and open hand strikes, utilized by all hsing-i practitioners. It is a middle-distance system, shorter than chang chuan but longer than wing chun.

The Foundation Stance

The footwork is based on one primary stance, called *san tsai shih* or "three essentials" stance. Sometimes referred to as a 30-70 posture, san tsai shih requires the hsing-i student to lower his body by bending his knees. This causes his chi to sink down to the *tan tien* (area around the navel believed to be the center of internal strength). From there, he distributes 30 percent of his weight to his front leg and 70 percent to his rear leg.

Hsing-i postures, as demonstrated by San Francisco Sifu Tai, are based on one primary stance, *san tsai shih:* 30 percent of the weight is on the lead leg, 70 percent rests on the rear leg.

Sifu Adam Hsu in a low hsing-i stance with his hands in a regular closed fist. Hsing-i combines direct linear strikes with secure and practical footwork.

This stance is the foundation stance of hsing-i. It is the most often-used fighting position and it provides the hsing-i practitioner with a strong sense of security and confidence. From this stance, the hsing-i practitioner can see and be in a position to react quickly to each move his opponent makes.

The footwork itself involves a short, level, and flat-moving half-step. Although it looks limited, it has a sound basis for its use. Most fighting consists of constant jockeying back and forth, shifting in close and then out of range. These are mostly half-steps. With its half-step footwork, hsing-i teaches its students how to make those critical adjustments.

The forms or sets follow a learning order. The first is called *wu hsing lien huan chuan* (five elements linking fist), and is the study of the five elements. This form provides basic training in fists and footwork. After that, the hsing-i student learns the twelve animal forms. These forms take a long time to perfect, since each animal has something differ-ent to contribute to the hsing-i practitioner's knowledge.

The final and most advanced level of hsing-i deals with the delivery of *hua chin* (*fa ging* in Cantonese), where the hsing-i stylist emits power without apparent physical force. This advanced level can also be called a form of *chi kung* and is strictly internal energy. There are only a few teachers of this art alive today.

Hsing-i weapons include the broadsword, double-edged sword, staff, and spear. They are, as with the empty-hand forms, simple and practical. There are no elaborate sword or staff circular techniques that are common-ly seen in other kung fu systems.

Hsing-i contains two man push-hand sparring which increases sensitivity, im-proves balance, and gives the hsing-i practi-tioner the opportunity to practice his tech-niques. Hsing-i push hands waste no time on flowing circular movements like those commonly used in tai chi and pa kwa. Tech-niques are quick, direct, and straightforward.

Pa Kwa
A Fighting Strategy in Eight Directions

By "walking the circle," the pa kwa practitioner learns the eight different angles of attack; his opponent only learns that a penetrating strike may come from anywhere.

"It's a game of strategy."

"It's like a puzzle, it makes you think. The more you get into it, the more you see and understand fighting tactics."

"It is a piece of art that the student never finishes."

These statements all describe pa kwa, a kung fu system known for its strong training and coupling of the student's internal energy with his external power.

Pa kwa means "eight directions." Thought by some to represent the eight trigram, or eight changes of *I-Ching* philosophy, pa kwa is more accurately defined as eight different angles of attack. The pa kwa system is geared toward training the kung fu practitioner to use those eight angles or directions.

Pa kwa originated toward the end of the Ching dynasty (about 1900). It was founded by Hai Chuan Tung, a renowned martial artist of that period.

Pa kwa has the reputation of being strictly an internal kung fu system, of employing chi in mysterious and subtle eight-step and eight-palm combinations that defeat the opponent with its flowing soft movements. Actually, as with most of the Northern Chinese kung fu systems, pa kwa initially teaches the student the soft or internal aspects of the art. Much time is spent with these soft techniques. They give the student flexibility and teach him how to use his entire body as a natural weapon. Originally, there was no need to teach pa kwa quickly, so training of the hard power or *ging* came later when the student understood the soft phase of his training.

As with tai chi chuan, many students didn't

advance to the external stage of their training, but still became teachers of pa kwa. To them, the soft form was the entire system, and pa kwa gained the reputation of being strictly an internal martial art.

Again like tai chi, the level of internal training in pa kwa is high, but it still takes some hard ging to cause damage to the enemy. What makes pa kwa an advanced kung fu system is that it combines internal and external strengths to produce a high level of fighting expertise. The so-called external systems are effective against street fighters. But martial arts such as pa kwa are designed to provide the advanced training and knowledge necessary to fight opponents who are also highly-trained fighters. This kind of training takes a lot of time and patience, but the end result is an advanced understanding of the blending of internal and external strengths.

The Pa Kwa Circle

Pa kwa practitioners spend a great deal of time learning the pa kwa circle or curve steps. They walk a continuous circle while constantly focusing their intent upon an unseen opponent, a practice that teaches the student how to move effectively. When fighting, the martial artist has two main areas to protect: the body (called the "big door" in pa kwa) and the shoulder and arm (small door). Most people instinctively want to protect their bodies. The arm and shoulder then become a side-door entrance to the attacking pa kwa practitioner. If he gets through the defense of this side-door, he will either reach his opponent's body or cause him to move away. Learning the eight directions of the pa kwa circle teaches him to attack from any angle. However he won't always attack his

opponent's sidedoor, since another feature of pa kwa is that it is always changing. The opposition doesn't know from where the pa kwa stylist will launch his attack.

The hand techniques emphasize penetration when striking. The pa kwa practitioner uses a twisting motion called *tzan sz jin* (reeling silk) to deliver power. This requires a loose supple waist. Open hand techniques are the most important hand strikes in pa kwa.

Palms Preferred

It is estimated that 90 percent of the hand techniques while training are palms, and 80 percent palms in actual fighting situations. Pa kwa practitioners believe that to make a fist automatically tightens the whole arm, and they want the arm relaxed, until the moment of impact. So, they prefer an open hand strike. Also, it's easier to deliver open hand strikes to localized points of the opponent's body, and do more damage.

Pa kwa doesn't emphasize stance training as do some other kung fu systems. Many styles stress strong, solid stances, since they contain a lot of body contact while fighting. The pa kwa stylist is always shifting and moving away to catch the opponent off-balance, so he doesn't need a solid low stance. He needs to remain more upright, in order to use his footwork and to attack from any angle. Pa kwa kicks are all low and practical. Again, the pa kwa stylist doesn't want to risk losing his balance or the ability to move quickly.

The Weapons

The system contains all four major traditional Chinese weapons (staff, spear, broadsword, and double-edged sword), as well as a few more. Double weapons are very popular in pa kwa, because the art utilizes both hands equally, unlike some kung fu systems, where one side is used to block and the other to strike.

Several weapons are considered pa kwa weapons. These are: the deer horn knife (*lu jyau do*), two crescent-shaped knife blades, crossed, with the grip on one side; and *pun gung bi,* a four-to-six-inch-long needle, sharp at both ends, that attaches to the middle finger with a ring. Both of these weapons are for close-in fighting and can easily be concealed on the pa kwa practitioner's body.

The Dummy

The pa kwa wooden dummy is more like a wooden post than a dummy. However, it can be used to perfect many pa kwa techniques.

Pa kwa contains two-man forms and, of course, free style sparring is important: it gives the pa kwa practitioner the opportunity to discover that pa kwa is an endless array of different technique combinations and fighting theories.

Tai Chi Chuan
The Yin and Yang of Combat

Although often considered a yoga-like exercise, tai chi blends soft, flowing *yin* strength with hard, fast, *yang* power to become an effective fighting art.

The two words, tai chi, describe the Chinese symbol for yin and yang. The tai chi symbol represents the Chinese belief that all life contains a blending of positive yang forces and negative yin power. Yang represents positive, light, active, male energy, and yin is negative, dark, cool, gentle, female strength. According to ancient Chinese writings, life cannot exist without a blending of these two forces. Yang continuously flows into and becomes yin and vice versa.

Tai chi chuan uses the yin and yang theory to form a high-level internal martial art. Although the general public often sees tai chi as a yoga-like exercise, it is really a separate kung fu system. The beginning training is misleading, because the first stage is soft, relaxed, and slow. It takes longer to attain the advanced level in tai chi than in other kung fu

styles, so most people aren't exposed to the final stage. The highest level of tai chi combines hard, fast power with soft flowing strength to produce a fighting art.

The Origins of the Art

One popular legend credits the origination of tai chi chuan to a Taoist priest of the early Yuan dynasty named Jang San Feng.

Jang San Feng learned his martial art in the Shaolin temple. One day, he sat next to a window pondering the thought that most martial arts systems used too much strength and heavy breathing, which was not good when combined with Taoist practice. As he sat thinking, he noticed a bird and a snake engaged in a fight to the death, outside his window. Jang was impressed with how relaxed both animals were and how the bird

was sometimes soft and gentle and sometimes soft and hard, but always quick. He observed that the snake was similar, sometimes slow, sometimes quick, but always a combination of soft and hard power with light relaxed breathing. From this observation, Jang San Feng developed tai chi chuan.

Other tai chi chuan historians credit the beginnings of the art to the Chen family of the Chen village in Northern China, around the end of the Sung dynasty and beginning of the Yuan dynasty. They believe that tai chi was taught to residents of the Chen village only, and kept a closely guarded secret by the Chen family.

We will probably never know for sure the truth about tai chi's beginnings, but it is certain that the current tai chi systems originated from the forms from the Chen village.

Chen style tai chi contained two forms, called the old form and the new form. Yang Lu Chan was an outsider who succeeded in learning Chen tai chi from Chen Chang Shing of the Chen family. Yang learned the old form. He taught it to his grandson, Yang Cheng Fu, and also was the first to teach Chen tai chi to outsiders. Yang Cheng Fu traveled throughout Northern and Southern China teaching tai chi. Many of the Chen tai chi movements were difficult kicks and hard external actions, not suitable for the old or infirm to practice. Yang Cheng Fu revised the Chen form into a softer tai chi form that all people could practice and benefit from. That form became Yang style tai chi, named after Yang Cheng Fu.

A martial artist named Wu Chuen You studied Chen tai chi from Yang Lu Chan's

Preceding pages: a wushu team performs chen style tai chi chuan, the oldest tai chi style. Though often thought a soft art, chen style has many hard and fast movements. Above: Sifu Y.C. Chiang leads his class in tai chi standing meditation form.

The tai chi practitioner flows with his opponent's strength until he finds an opening, and then strikes with hard external force.

eldest son, Yang Ban Ho. Wu had originally studied *shuai-jao* (Chinese wrestling), so he added more throwing and locking techniques to Chen tai chi and developed the Wu style tai chi.

There is also a seldom seen style known as Sun style tai chi, founded by Sun Lok Tang, a master of hsing-i and pa kwa. Sun combined many hsing-i and pa kwa movements into his tai chi style.

The differences between the three major tai chi chuan styles are: 1) Chen contains hard as well as soft techniques, some resembling regular kung fu with fast hard power and footwork; 2) Yang is made up of large graceful circles, and the techniques are easy to see and understand; 3) Wu uses smaller circles with more throwing and pushing techniques.

However, no matter what style, all tai chi chuan contains both hard and soft movements. Soft is taught first, to develop the student's internal strength and flexibilty. The next level is training for the fast hard power necessary to damage the opponent. The final stage is a combination of hard and soft, which allows the tai chi practitioner to blend soft techniques with hard power. He does this by flowing with his opponent's strength until he finds an opening, and then striking with hard external yang force.

The Thirteen Principles

There are 13 principle techniques common to all tai chi styles. They are broken down into eight hand techniques and five directions of footwork. The eight hand techniqes are—

1) *peng*—ward off
2) *lu*—roll back
3) *gi*—press
4) *on*—push
5) *tsai*—pull
6) *li*—twist
7) *tzao*—elbow
8) *kau*—lean

The five directions of footwork are—

1) *jun*—center
2) *toy*—left
3) *gow*—right
4) *pon*—front
5) *ding*—back

Push Hands

It is said by tai chi practitioners that, "The individual forms are learned in order to learn and understand oneself. Tai chi *toy sao* (push hands) are necessary to know and understand the other person."

There are two kinds of push hands; single toy sao and double-handed toy sao. Toy sao exercises develop four stages of power. The first is *ting ging* and is translated to "listen to force." Ting ging means that the tai chi practitioner learns to feel his opponent's next move rather than see it. The next stage is *dong ging,* which means to understand and to know the opponent's force. Third is *fa ging,* where the tai chi stylist learns to dissolve his adversary's force. The fourth and final level of tai chi ging is called *fat ging.* Here the tai chi practitioner has learned how to release his own ging, his attacking force.

The basic features of tai chi chuan, which make it unique, are: power comes from the waist, but the whole body is relaxed; the elbows are always relaxed and down, not up or out; the shoulders are always dropped down; the hips are tucked in, under the practitioner's center of gravity; and the chest is relaxed and concave.

These five important basics all promote excellent internal and external conditioning and good all-around health. They give the tai chi chuan practitioner his source of power for both internal and external ging.

Chen Xiaowing demonstrates the chen "single whip posture." Right: Kai Ying Tung, a master of yang style tai chi, with the tai chi sword, a narrow, flexible sword taught only to, and used by, advanced students. Overleaf: In tai chi the hands "listen to"—and control—one's opponent.

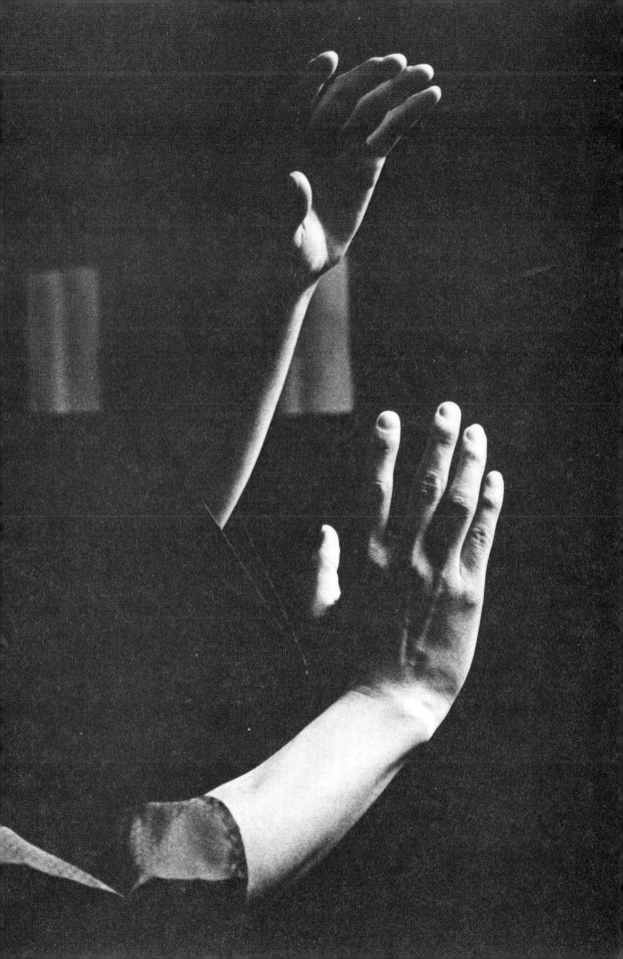

Bow Sim Mark assumes the posture known as
"grasp the bird's tail."

Southern Kung Fu: Five Fighting Families

Originally, there were five principle Southern kung fu systems. They were designated by the word *gar* following the founder's name. Gar means family, and, in this case, stands for kung fu families.

The five family systems were originated strictly as fighting arts, used to battle the Ching dynasty rulers. Unlike Northern systems, which were older and had evolved during peaceful times when students could study their martial arts for years before reaching higher levels, the masters of the Southern systems had to hurry their training and quickly teach their students how to fight. As a result, hard power was taught first, followed by internal training. Stances were wider and lower, and Southern footwork less active than Northern, relying more on the practitioner's strength for defense.

The families were:

1) *Hung gar*—Founded by Hung Hei Gung, it uses external strength and dynamic tension exercises and is excellent for developing muscles and strong low stances.

2) *Lau gar*—Founded by Lau Sqam Ngan, it is a middle-length hand system, not often taught in present times.

3) *Choy gar*—No relation to choy-li-fut, the system was founded by Choy Gau Yee and is a long-arm style.

4) *Li Gar*—Founded by Li Yao San (also one of choy-li-fut's originators), this seldom-taught system features a strong medium-range fist.

5) *Mok gar*—Founded by Mok Ching Giu, who was famous in Canton for his powerful kicks, this system places emphasis on short-hand techniques and strong kicks.

With the exception of hung gar, the Southern family styles are rarely seen today in their original forms. Most of the popular Southern systems, including choy-li-fut, wing chun, and white crane, had their roots in the Shaolin temple martial system, or in other Northern styles. When escaping revolutionaries transplanted these arts to Southern China, they adopted many of the distinguishing characteristics of the native styles. The combination of Northern and Southern elements make these kung fu systems particularly versatile and effective self-defense systems.

蔡李佛

Choy-Li-Fut
The Fist at the End of the Rope

One of the most powerful kung fu styles, choy li-fut is famous for its long-arm technique: granite fists whipped through the air at the end of loose and supple arms.

One of the most popular kung fu systems in Asia—practiced by one third of the martial artists in Hong Kong—choy-li-fut kung fu is famous for its combination of hard and soft techniques, speed, and balance with power and extension. Not only does the style contain a vast variety of hand and weapons forms, but many of the top full-contact tournament fighters in Southeast Asia are choy-li-fut practitioners, a fact that supports the art's reputation as one of the most powerful kung fu styles in existence.

Choy-li-fut was founded in 1836 by a martial artist named Chan Heung. Chan Heung learned kung fu from Shaolin temple martial artists, including a well-known fighting monk named Choy Fook. After spending over 20 years perfecting his kung fu, Chan Heung returned to his village to put together a new fighting system that would soon become famous as a revolutionary force. It was named choy-li-fut in honor of Chan Heung's teachers. The word *fut,* which means Buddha in Chinese, paid respect to the Shaolin temple roots of the new kung fu system.

At this time, the Manchurians of the Ching dynasty ruled China. The Ching were corrupt rulers, and soon rebel forces developed

Left: Sifu Doc Fai Wong, one of the highest-ranking sifus in the US, with the rare choy-li-fut weapon called the nine dragon trident (a weapon favored by Chan Heung, choy-li-fut's creator). Right: Tat Mau Wong (top) and Lee Koon Hung (below) demonstrate the flexible waist and extended arms that, with low stances, are characteristic of choy-li-fut kung fu.

among the oppressed Chinese people. Chan Heung found it impossible not to become involved. He began training men in the art of choy-li-fut to fight the Imperial army of the Manchurians. Chan Heung's system became a secret society, a revolutionary fighting system.

Although choy-li-fut is referred to as a Southern kung fu system because it originated in Kwang Tung, Southern China, one of Chan Heung's teachers, the monk Choy Fook, came from the Northern Shaolin temple. Choy-li-fut is actually a combination of Northern and Southern styles. It employs the relaxed circular long arm movements and footwork of the North, combined with the power and low stances characteristic of Southern Chinese kung fu.

The Body as Rope Dart

The power of choy-li-fut comes from a balanced stance which uses the hip as a motor, causing the waist to turn with each movement. Choy-li-fut derives much of its famous long arm power from a loose supple wasit and shoulders. This type of power is sometimes compared to the ancient Chinese weapon, the rope dart. The waist is like the hand throwing the rope dart, strong but flexible. The choy-li-fut practitioner's arm becomes the rope itself, light, loose, and supple. Finally, his fist is like the dart on the end of the rope, a strong solid power.

Choy-li-fut contains both long and short hand movements within the system. Extension is important for fighting more than one opponent at a time and for long-range strikes. The long arm techniques are for power and extension, and the short hands for close-in fighting, using the elbows, knees, and wrists.

There are four principle fists around which most of the choy-li-fut offense hand techniques are structured.

1) *Tsop* is a straight punch using the second digits of the hand as the striking surface. This gives the punch a two-inch-longer extension and more focus.

2) *Qua* is a back fist or back knuckle using the whole body as the driving force. The choy-li-fut practitioner's hips and shoulders move in a circular manner to produce the maximum power.

3) *Jong* is an uppercut, again using extension and complete body and waist movement for power.

4) *Sow* is the trademark punch of the choy-li-fut system. It's like a roundhouse punch, and it is the knockout punch of choy-li-fut. Full waist and hip action is always employed with the sow. Two hands are often used in combination with this punch, one hand for a qua or back fist and the other a split second later with the sow.

The choy-li-fut system contains animal forms, such as the snake, crane, tiger, dragon, and leopard. The style also uses elbows, knees, sweeps, takedowns, and many grappling techniques. For the advanced student, there are pressure point strikes using the knuckles and fingertips.

Choy-li-fut has a vast arsenal of forms— over 100—available to learn. Most people specialize in whichever sets fit their ability and personality. Some forms are external and some internal. The external forms are a harder and faster style, designed to condition and benefit muscle and bone, and increase the stamina of the practitioner. The internal sets are slow, even, flowing, and relaxed. They promote internal organ harmony, are good for improving health, and build chi, the source of internal energy. Choy-li-fut starts with external training. When the student has entered the advanced phase of his training, he learns the internal aspects of the art.

Arsenal of Weapons

Choy-li-fut has many more weapons within its structure than most other kung fu styles. The two primary weapons of the system are

Preceding pages: Two students perform a kwan-do ("General Kwan's knife") vs. spear routine during a Chinese New Year celebration. Right: Doc Fai Wong wields a three-section staff, one of choy-li-fut's deadliest weapons.

Many of the top full-contact tournament fighters in Southeast Asia are choy-li-fut practitioners . . .

the butterfly knives and the staff. Weapons in choy-li-fut are broken down into four categories: long, short, flexible, and double weapons. Among the long weapons are the staff, spear, kwon-do (long-handled knife), monk's shovel, farmer's hoe, and trident. Short weapons include the broadsword, double-edged sword, umbrella, fan, and cane. In the flexible category, are the chain whip and three-sectioned staff. Double weapons are double-broadswords, butterfly knives, battle axes, double daggers, double chain whips, and double hook swords.

One weapon unique to the choy-li-fut system is the nine-dragon trident. This is a long heavy weapon with a series of half moon-shaped hooks at the end, protruding in four directions. The nine-dragon trident was said to have been the personal weapon of choy-li-fut's founder, Chan Heung.

The empty hand forms of the choy-li-fut system give the student a solid background in the system's techniques. Each move in each set has a specific defensive or offensive meaning. The forms average 100 to 150 moves, with some up to 300 moves. Choy-li-fut's hand and weapon sets are longer than those of most other kung fu systems. Besides teaching choy-li-fut techniques and power, the forms are beneficial as training aids for stamina and conditioning.

Choy-li-fut contains many two-man forms, both empty hand and with weapons. These teach the student timing and distance, and are popular with spectators at kung fu exhibitions, both in the United States and in the Orient.

Lion dancing is another important segment of choy-li-fut. Traditionally, lion dancing is performed at Chinese holiday festivities and is the opening ceremony for kung fu demonstrations.

Choy-li-fut is famous for its large variety of wooden dummy training aids. The system contains over eight different dummies, all with their own purpose. The *ching jong* dummy is the most popular, but there is also a sandbag dummy, a dummy called *ba kwa jong* for staff training, one used for pressure point and fan strike, and a spring base dummy for practicing kicks. The wagon dummy has wheels and rolls slowly when hit, and the bamboo-growth dummy will toughen students' arms.

杏家

Hung Gar
Hard As Iron . . . Soft As Thread

Wide low stances; slow but powerful strikes; and a tradition of advanced internal training make hung gar a formidable self-defense system.

Hung gar kung fu is a child of the Shaolin temple of Fukien in Southern China. Its founder, Hung Hei Gune, learned his art from the Shaolin monk, Gee Shimn Sien See, who was an expert in the *fu jao* (tiger fist) system. The most famous master of hung gar was Wong Fei Hung, who has been the subject of many Chinese kung fu movies.

Hung gar is one of the most popular Southern Chinese systems. It fits all body structures and is good for students of all ages. It is a slower system than some other styles, Northern Shaolin for instance, but that is due partly to the fact that the stances are much wider and lower than in many other kung fu systems. Hung gar is known for its strong stances and powerful hand techniques. It is especially good for developing strength, both in legs and arms. The training consists of prolonged stance training and many isometric breathing exercises which are incorporated into the sets.

The hung gar practitioner learns to create strong solid power, originating from the hips and the low solid stances. He doesn't move as much as do those practitioners of some other kung fu systems, but when he connects, his fist has a punishing impact on his opponent. The isometric and dynamic tension exercises inherent in the hung gar forms bring about a certain amount of internal energy, which when coupled with the external power, make him a formidable opponent.

From Tiger Fists to Iron Threads

The hung gar student also learns a set called "cross tiger fist" *(gung gee fook fu)* which strengthens his body and teaches him how to breathe. This is the oldest form in the hung gar system. It was originated by the founder, Hung Hei Gung.

For the more advanced student, there is the "ten forms" set *(sup ying)* which includes the five animals—tiger, crane, dragon, leop-

ard, and snake; and the five elements—metal, wood, fire, water, and earth. The animal forms teach the hung gar student power and spirit. The elements are more abstract. One element can counter one other element. So the elements give the student of hung gar a foundation of useful techniques against any attack.

Although hung gar looks like an external style, it enters the sphere of internal training through its "iron thread" *(tit sien)* form. The iron thread set is used for chi and stance training. It contains the movements of the dragon. It is the most advanced form of the system, and if practiced by a beginner, it can seriously injure the student. It is named iron thread because the techniques are partly as "hard as iron" and partly as "soft as thread." The form follows the yin and yang principle of hard and soft blending into a perfect balance and harmony.

Moral Rectitude

Hung gar is a straightforward, honest style with a strong philosophy that teaches the student to use self-control and to use his kung fu knowledge properly. This philosophy can be found written in Chinese characters in most hung gar schools. It's one of the reasons that Wong Fei Hung was so popular in the Chinese martial arts world. He was a firm believer in doing only that which is morally correct, and traditional hung gar schools have adhered to that belief.

Hung gar contains all of the weapons common to Southern Chinese kung fu. One weapon for which the style is well-known is the trident or "tiger fork," a long-handled weapon with a three-pronged fork at the end. Hung gar is also famous for its single-ended staff set *(ng long bat kwa quen)* and for its butterfly knife form *(ji ma do)*. Among the many other weapons in the hung gar system are the double-chain whips, broadsword, spear, and kwon do (long handled knife).

Because of its versatility and health features, hung gar is becoming increasingly popular in the United States. Many fine hung gar sifu have come to the United States to teach their martial art.

Wing Chun
The Shortest Distance Between Two Points

Practitioners of this direct, aggressive self-defense style waste no time in getting to the point—short, straight strikes right to the centerline of their opponent's body.

Wing chun kung fu, the only system believed to have been founded by a woman, is an aggressive style that is used strictly for self-defense.

The legend relates that a girl named Yim Wing Chun desired to learn martial arts at the Shaolin temple. She caught the attention of a Shaolin nun named Ng Mui, who was an accomplished martial artist. So impressed was Ng Mui with Yim Wing Chun's ability and desire, that she offered to teach Shaolin martial arts to her. The kung fu that Yim Wing Chun learned consisted of only three forms, instead of the ten or more taught in other Shaolin systems. Her kung fu was also used only for self-defense and lacked the fancy sets that other styles used to entice potential martial artists into the kung fu systems. Yim Wing Chun's style consisted of short direct movements designed to eliminate any wast-

ed energy and to encourage speed in the counterattacks. It also included training with wooden dummies and *chi sao* (sticky hand) techniques.

There are several different types of wing chun within the system. The most popular and common style seen today is the "slant body" form practiced by Bruce Lee and his famous sifu Yip Man, who was considered the grandmaster of modern wing chun. There also exists a type called "side body" wing chun originated by sifu Fong Sun, and *pao fa lein* wing chun founded by Liu Ta-Sheng.

While Yip Man's wing chun contains only three hand forms and one wooden dummy set, the pao fa lein style consists of ten hand forms and four wooden dummy forms.

No Wasted Effort

A highly aggressive art, wing chun concen-

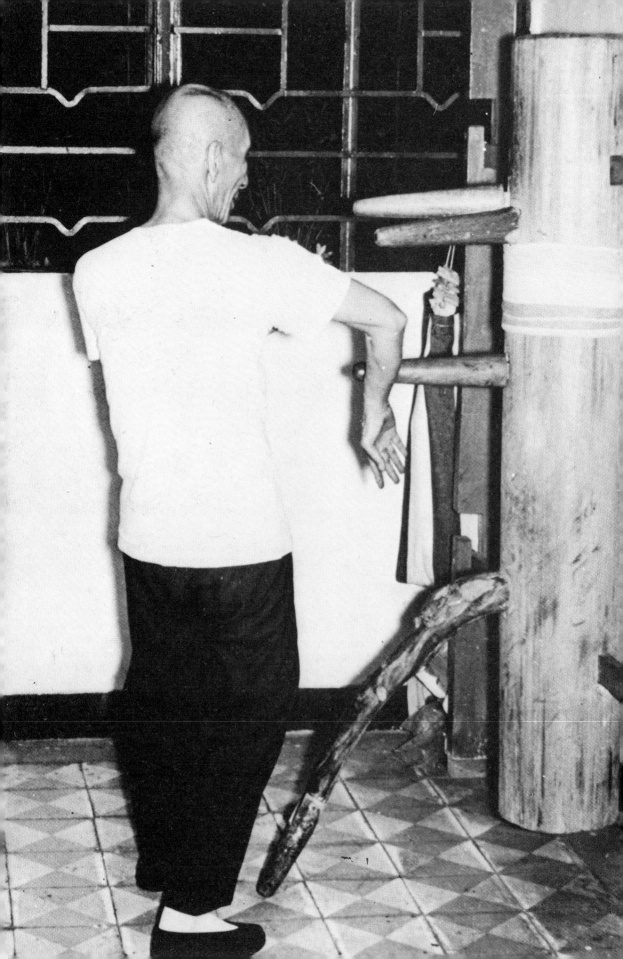

Left and above: the famed Yip Man (1884-1972), the last grandmaster of wing chun and the father of the modern version. At left he works on the *mook jong* or "wooden man"; above, with his students. Yip Man's most famous pupil was Bruce Lee.

trates on centerline attacks, using no wasted effort. Blocks are used to redirect the opponent's strike so that the wing chun practitioner can counterattack with either his blocking hand or the other hand, in a very close-in position. Since the shortest distance between two points is a straight line, there are no circular movements to be seen in most wing chun styles. (An exception is again pao fa lein, which is based upon short fluid circular movements.)

Attacking-hand movements in the wing chun system are of the short one-inch punch type made famous by the late Bruce Lee and are all delivered along the centerline of the opponent's body. There are also many knee, elbow, and finger attacks. Sixty percent of attacking techniques are hand techniques and the other 40 percent is comprised of short low kicks. Hand and foot techniques are delivered simultaneously in the wing chun system. All wing chun techniques are perfected on the wing chun dummy *(mook jong)*. This dummy consists of two arms and a midsection projection for practicing hand techniques; and a leg against which the eight types of quick low kicks are practiced.

The wooden dummy allows the wing chun student the opportunity to use his full force and power, while at the same time toughening the bones and muscles in his arms and legs. Wing chun uses the wooden dummy more than other kung fu systems.

Sticky Hands

Chi sao (sticky hands) is a unique training feature of the wing chun system. In chi sao practice two wing chun practitioners face each other and move their wrists and forearms against each other's wrists and forearms in small circles. The sensitivity developed in the wrists and forearms by this practice allows the wing chun stylist to predict the opponent's next move. He is also so close in to his opponent that he can use his chi sao technique to counter and attack instantly. The practitioner uses the short quick movements of chi sao to his best advantage, striking before his opponent realizes where the attack is coming from.

Wing chun kung fu contains few weapons. The most famous weapons of its arsenal are the staff and the butterfly knives. The pao fa lein wing chun style, however, contains many more weapons. The broadsword, butterfly knives, trident, and staff are just a few of the weapons available in pao fa lein wing chun.

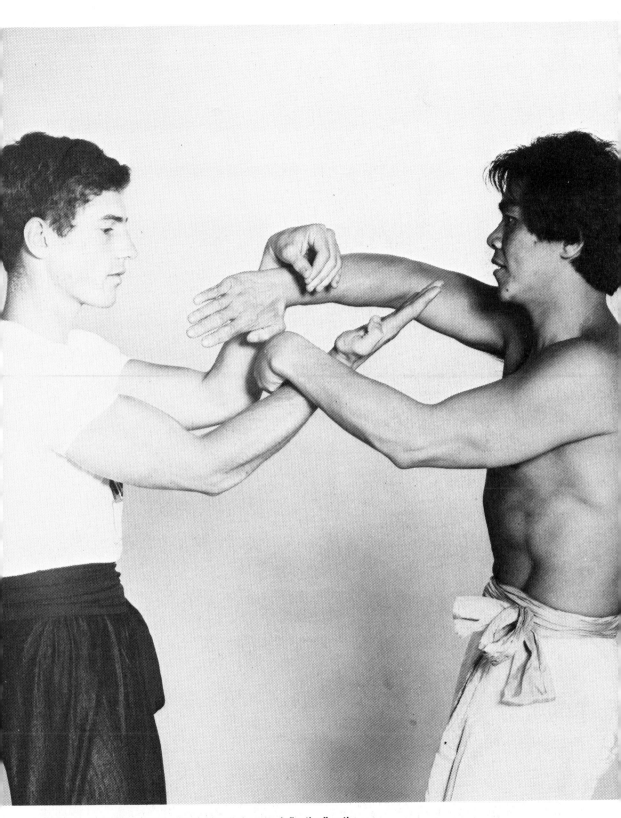

Left: Sifu Leo Whang executes a *bong sao* or "wing arm deflection" on the mook jong. Above: William (Chuk Hing) Cheung (right), one of Yip Man's surviving students, shows the use of *chi sao,* in which the defender's wrists and forearms stay in contact with those of his opponent, allowing him to "read" the enemy's every move.

西藏白鶴

Tibetan White Crane
One Hand Lies, One Hand Tells the Truth

Balanced by his widespread "wings," the white crane stylist launches devastating blows with his two powerful "beaks." The crane's light-footed and evasive movements make sure he will never be hit in return.

The elegant crane positions himself on one leg, his wings outstretched for balance and to prepare for an attack from a small but ferocious fox. The fox leaps; the crane feints to one side and brings one huge wing down upon his attacker's head.

This description could be of the defense tactics of the regal white crane from a lakeside scene in Northern China; it also depicts a unique style of Chinese kung fu.

White crane kung fu came to China several hundred years ago from the Western section of the Chinese Empire. Sometimes known as Llama or Tibetan white crane, the system was originally developed in the West, then adopted and cultivated by the people of Southern China. And when white crane became popular in the South, it lost none of the circling footwork and high kicks that resemble those of the Northern styles.

White crane kung fu has in the past been taught only to select students; masters of the system are known for their care taken in choosing only the right students to accept for training. In Asia, guns are not as common as in the United States, so the Chinese gangster often has to rely on empty hand fighting. Honorable kung fu systems such as white crane have developed a tradition of refusing to teach disreputable people. Since kung fu can be a deadly martial art in the wrong hands, masters believe that to teach it to the wrong people is to do a disservice to society.

White crane master
Ngai Yoh Tong
stands with his
students in a regal
crane stance with
hands in pecking
position ready to
strike.

White crane (*bak hok* in Cantonese) is often referred to as a completely defensive kung fu system, because the white crane practitioner never initiates an attack. He will always wait for his opponent to attack, then he evades and counterattacks.

Taught never to use force against force, the white crane practitioner uses what is referred to as "revolving force," the art of using the opponent's own force against himself. The crane stylist utilizes the system's footwork and crane-like postures to lure his enemy into a vulnerable position, then counterattacks mercilessly.

Two Angry Beaks

White crane is known as a long-arm style, and it is truly that. The outstretched arms of the crane practitioner end in fists resembling beaks of angry cranes. While one fist is used for striking, the other is kept outstretched to maintain balance and to use against the opponent in case another blow is needed. This is a basic principle of the white crane system. Called "one hand lies and one hand tells the truth," it means that one hand is a diversion and the other hand is the actual striking hand. Of course, the enemy doesn't know which is which, and the white crane practitioner can easily switch from one hand to another.

The crane stylist might face his attacker at an angle, always maintaining an arms-width distance. When the opponent attacks, the white crane will step aside to redirect the antagonist's fist and counterattack at almost the same instant, using his body and waist to obtain maximum power. The amount of power derived from the whole arm length and the action of the waist, hips, and back muscles produces the same effect as being hit by a sledge hammer.

Where the wing chun practitioner might encourage the sticky hand contact known as chi sao, the white crane stylist allows no contact at all. The force generated by using the whole arm and body requires distance between the crane practitioner and his opponent. He can't allow his enemy to get close enought to get inside his reach and attack his weak areas. He must strike quickly and with enough power to end the fight, before his opponent can reach him.

The crane stylists feel they have an advantage with their long-arm attacks. Their arms become an extension of their bodies. When a white crane practitioner strikes, the power behind that strike comes from his hips and waist with a twisting, almost corkscrew motion of his body. There is no push-pull of his fists as in some of the Japanese martial arts. Also, he uses no recoil, since his arms are already outstretched. His fist becomes a missile and his body the launching force.

The Four Fists

There are four basic fists taught in white crane, each one an important trademark of the system.

1) *Chuin* is an ultra-fast straight punch. Speed is very important in crane kung fu, because the crane stylist has a longer distance to travel with his long fist before contact is made with his opponent. Chuin is the fastest of the white crane basic fists.

2) *Pow* is the crane stylist's strongest strike. It is an uppercut and often serves as a block against the attacker's punch, and then turns into a strike against the attacker. The crane practitioner puts power into this punch with his whole body.

3) *Kup* is a revolving circular overhead strike. Here again, the crane stylist uses his whole body to collect and distribute the force of this strike.

4) *Chow* is a roundhouse punch with the knuckles used as the striking surface.

Ever-Shifting Footwork

White crane footwork is similar to Northern Chinese kung fu systems. The crane stylist moves constantly, never remaining in one position long enough for his opponent to reach him. The stances are very low, with the crane practitioner's weight placed mainly on

White crane emphasizes the use of angles in fighting. Gary Fung above uses angles to avoid his opponent while striking back to the opponent's face.

Unlike other kung fu systems which use high kicks for training but only low kicks in combat, white crane uses high powerful kicks in fighting, as demonstrated here by Raymond Mak.

his front foot. The back foot is used to change position.

The footwork involves a circling technique common with many Northern systems, such as pa kwa. The white crane circles his opponent looking for an opening in his assailant's defense. This circling footwork gives him flexibility in his own movements and often confuses his opponent. His attacker isn't sure where the crane will be next, or what he'll do, so is forced to follow the crane stylist. A perfect situation evolves, where the assailant attacks in confusion, and the elusive crane counterattacks against the now off-balance opponent. The footwork associated with this circling maneuver is called the goose stance, because it is a very low and solid stance.

Some Northern kung fu systems, chang chuan for instance, have substantial amounts of high kicks, which are performed high for practice only. In actual fighting the chang chuan practitioner kicks low to preserve his

balance. This is not the case with white crane. The crane stylist often kicks high and with great speed. He is able to maintain his balance easily because he uses his outstretched arms to balance himself. There are also low kicks, and one of the most frequently used low kicks is a powerful side kick. Most of the time a kick is used in conjunction with a lightning-fast fist attack.

White crane kung fu is very much like the aggressive fighting attitude of its avian counterpart. When fighting, the white crane practitioner considers himself very dangerous, much more dangerous than his enemy. Therefore, he cannot be beaten. This is the essence of the white crane style.

It should be noted that in more recent history, two sister systems, llama and hop gar kung fu, have evolved and are frequently described under the name white crane. They are very similar to and have the same origins as Tibetan white crane.

白眉毛

White Eyebrow
Soft Hands and Scared Power

At first, his confused opponent only knows that soft hand movements are guiding away all of his intended blows; suddenly, one of his weak points is struck with explosive, damaging force. The white eyebrow stylist walks away, having once again demonstrated his "wit."

The Taoist priest had totally white hair, including his eyebrows. He was called Bak Mei, which means "white eyebrow" in Cantonese.

Bak Mei was one of a group of revolutionaries seeking to overthrow the Manchurian rulers of China during the Ching dynasty. It was decided that one member of this group should infiltrate the royal palace and spy for the revolutionaries. Bak Mei was chosen for the task, but unfortunately, both the revolution and their infiltration were unsuccessful. Bak Mei, to escape certain death from the Man-

chus, became a traitor to the revolutionary cause and joined the forces of the Ching. He taught his kung fu style, named bak mei, to many members of the Ching and gained followers in Northern China. Meanwhile, the Southerners turned against him for betraying his fellow revolutionaries. At that time, bak mei kung fu was known by only a few Taoist and Buddhist monks, and they were reluctant to teach a traitor's art.

Finally a monk named Jok Fat received permission from his sifu, Gong Wei, to teach white eyebrow. Jok Fat wandered throughout

goes into developing power or *ging.* When executing a punch, the eyes, mind, hands, and feet must coordinate. To be proficient, one has to couple the external five forms with the internal five forms. The external five are: eyes *(ngan)*, mind *(sum)*, hands *(sau)*, waist *(yiu)*, and stance *(ma)*. The internal five are: spirit *(sun)*, purpose *(yee)*, courage *(gi)*, internal power *(chi)*, and power *(ging)*.

There are six sources of power in the hands and these are: *biu* (a thrust), *chum* (sink as if pushing a ball down into water), *tarn* (spring forward), *fa* (neutralize softly), and *tung* (an aggressive move, similar to a shark eating his prey). The *chuk* is released in a sharp sudden explosion that creates a great amount of force, since all of the person's chi

Left: So Kim Kwong shows white eyebrow kung fu. All strikes in this style are to vital pressure points; hand movements are soft until contact is made. Above: in white eyebrow footwork as the right or left leg moves forward the opposite arm is extended.

China looking for a suitable student. While in Canton, in Southern China, he found that student in the person of Cheung Lai Chuen. Chuen became the first student of white eyebrow kung fu in Southern China who was not a monk, and also became the first grandmaster of the white eyebrow system.

White eyebrow is usually referred to as a short, middle-hand system. The arms are flexible and soft until contact is made, then they are sharp and sudden with a penetrating power. The strength or power in white eyebrow is referred to as "sudden" or "scared" power, and unlike many other martial art's the white eyebrow practitioner's power is released only upon impact. Prior to actual impact, his hand movements are soft. The white eyebrow stylists derive much of their power and flexibility from waist action, more so than do some other short hand styles, such as wing chun.

Sources of Power

Much of the learning of white eyebrow

The white eyebrow practitioner only releases his sharp, sudden power upon contact with his opponent's vulnerable, empty areas.

or internal energy is behind it. Proper breathing is very important to delivering this power.

While a lot of soft power is used to redirect and guide the opponent's energy away from the white eyebrow stylist, it must be remembered that soft power cannot hit with force. For the actual strike, the white eyebrow practitioner quickly changes from soft to hard and strikes only at the weak points of his opponent's body. The six ging hand movements are all used in conjunction with one another, and the number of combinations is astronomical. White eyebrow is always looking for empty areas or openings in the opponent's defense. They only release their sharp sudden power upon contact with these vulnerable empty areas of the opposition's body.

Phoenix Eye

All of the strikes are to vital pressure points of the enemy's body. The only fist that white eyebrow uses is a phoenix eye fist. The phoenix eye, made with the first knuckle of the index finger extended, is much more effective than a regular fist, because the point of contact is condensed into that one index finger knuckle. It's like the difference between being hit by a spear point and a

hammer. The spear point is much more penetrating, while the hammer spreads the force outward.

The white eyebrow practitioner always waits for his opponent to attack first. Then he can tind his adversary's weak points. When he sees those weaknesses, he generates power and speed from his footwork and his twisting waist action. This, in turn, allows him to strike forcibly from only a few inches distance.

In order to bring forth power and gain inches for his punches, the white eyebrow stylist learns to "swallow his chest." This is a method of concentrating the expelled force in a quick and sudden manner. The white eyebrow practitioner rounds his shoulders and back, making his chest concave. When he strikes, he exhales his breath sharply, twists his waist to gain more power, and literally pushes the ging out with his waist, back, and shoulder action. The power is very much like a whip. His twisting waist applies all of the force from one side to the other. This action makes the power one-sided, but also gives the white eyebrow stylist a lot of stability.

White eyebrow footwork is referred to as "triangle footwork" and is designed to allow the white eyebrow practitioner to move aside quickly. His feet move in a triangle pattern, front to rear and side to side. And, if the left foot moves forward, the right hand is extended, and vice versa with the other side. This gives the white eyebrow stylist more stability.

Cleverness, or what white eyebrow practitioners call "wit," is very important to this system. Wit is the ability to quickly out-think and deceive the opponent. The white eyebrow practitioner's cleverness allows him to avoid the attacking blow and immediately counterattack.

There are eight hand forms in the white eyebrow system. The basic weapons are the chain-whip, trident, double-edged sword, butterfly knives, staff, and spear.

There is a traditional white eyebrow formula that describes the attitude of the bak mei practitioner. It lists the requirements of white eyebrow training in order of importance.

1) He must be clever in using his bak mei techniques.

2) He must be brave.

3) He must develop and perfect his bak mei techniques.

4) He must develop his strength.

Left: the phoenix eye fist is the *only* fist formation used in bak mei. Below: the white eyebrow practitioner must change his soft movement into explosive power in the last moment before his strike connects.

Esoteric Southern Styles

Choy mok's unique sticky hand techniques; hung fut's secret weapon—the shirt off the practitioner's back; dragon style's merciless fighting system based on a mythical beast's magical powers; the machine-gun-like attacks of southern praying mantis . . . these unusual arts share the distinction of being virtually unknown in North America. Nevertheless, the history of these arts and their effectiveness as fighting styles should give them a place in any survey of southern style kung fu. Here is a glimpse of some of the major features of these rare arts.

An instructor in Hong Kong demonstrates the low stance with open-handed claws that are the trademarks of choy mok.

Choy Mok: Seven Points of Power

Choy mok, a fairly recent kung fu system, founded a little over 50 years ago, combines the original southern family style, choy gar and mok gar. Choy mok contains both the short-range attacks of mok gar and the long-arm techniques of choy gar. However, the emphasis is placed on the short distance strikes. Close-in fighting techniques predominate in the choy mok system.

The stances are low, with the waist, back, and shoulders working as a unit to produce the power. Choy mok practitioners prefer to launch their attacks from solid stationary positions. Therefore, there isn't much active footwork in choy mok. Fists are used much more than kicks. Kicks are applied only for close-in fighting and are aimed at targets from the waist down.

Choy mok hand techniques can be either open hands or fists. Since so many short-hand movements are used, speed is important. Open hand strikes are frequently practiced to obtain speed in conversions from blocks to attacks.

The choy mok practitioner's favorite fist is the phoenix eye fist, and he always attaches a spiraling wrist action to his phoenix eye fist to obtain more power and concentrated force.

Although many of the hand techniques are short-distance strikes, the choy mok stylist combines them with small circular arm and shoulder movements to increase the striking force. This differs from other short-hand systems, such as wing chun, which employs more straight-line hand techniques. Elbow strikes are also popular in the choy mok system, and are again directed in a small circle pattern. The manner in which the choy mok practitioner uses small circles in his techniques allows him to easily change from

105

a block to a strike and vice-versa.

Choy mok training includes a chi sao-like exercise that is helpful in developing his sense of reflex feeling. This kind of chi sao is unique to choy mok. It teaches the choy mok student seven points of arm and wrist power. When the opponent touches one of these seven points, the choy mok practitioner reacts against him with power and control radiating from that point. Other systems with chi sao exercises (wing chun, white eyebrow, southern praying mantis) use the whole arm as the sensing and striking force. Choy mok's chi sao is strictly hard external power,

whereas other systems' chi sao are more internal and soft.

The choy mok system contains several weapons. The staff is the main weapon of the style. There are two types of choy mok staffs; one long and the other much shorter. The broadsword (don-do) and double broadsword are the principle short weapons. Choy mok also contains trident, kwon-do, and bench forms.

Hung Fut: The Left-Handed Strike

Hung fut is another hybrid system, which originated over 300 years ago as a combina-

Hung fut, a 300-year-old hybrid system combining hung gar and fut gar, is unique in its emphasis on striking first with the left hand.

tion of hung gar and fut gar kung fu. Hung gar's founder, Hung Hei Gung, had a student who was a Shaolin monk named Loy Yuen. Loy Yuen founded the fut gar system (Fut means Buddha in Cantonese). One of Loy Yuen's students, a monk called Chit Sin, combined hung gar and fut gar techniques into a new style which he called hung fut.

The techniques in hung fut look very similar to those of hung gar, except for one important feature. All hung fut practitioners strike first with their left hands. The idea behind this unique practice is that most people are right-handed and will attack initially with their right hands. When the hung fut stylist steps to the left of that right punch and blocks it, he has closed any opening for the attacker to use his own left hand as a follow-up punch. When the hung fut practitioner blocks, he pushes his opponent's right arm to the left, which forces the opposition's body to turn in that direction. From there, the adversary can't use his left hand to counterattack. Hung fut stylists also believe that to use the left hand first makes it easier to surprise and confuse the opposition.

Hand techniques are equally long and

Hung fut stylists believe that to use the left hand first makes it easier to surprise and confuse the opposition.

---

short arm with both fist and palm strikes. The *fu-jao* (tiger claw) is especially liked, since it can be easily changed from a palm strike to a fu-jao.

Footwork follows in the same order as hand techniques: The left foot always advances first. Stances are wide and low, just as with hung gar. Fifty percent of the movements are kicks and leg sweeps. Hung fut footwork moves in all four directions.

All single-handed weapons in the hung fut system are held in the left hand instead of the right hand. They are the same weapons that are seen in hung gar kung fu.

Another interesting feature of hung fut is that almost anything can be used as a weapon. There is a famous set originating from the system's founder called the "iron cloth form." In this set, the shirt off of the hung fut practitioner's back becomes the weapon. It's used like a whip, to catch the opponent, and then pull him off-balance.

Hung fut's power is developed from the stances and footwork. There is no waist action involved with generating power in hung fut kung fu. Like hung gar, the hung fut system uses dynamic tension exercises to develop strength and low stances for power and balance. Their type of power is referred to as hard *ging* or inch power, and is strictly external power.

Dragon: Total Submission of the Enemy

Kung fu is famous for its animal forms. All of the animals depicted in kung fu styles are actual living animals, with the exception of one. That exception is the little known dragon or *lung ying* system.

The dragon is reputed to be able to disappear and reappear at will and be able to reduce or magnify the size of its body. From this ancient heritage came the powerful dragon style kung fu. The way of the dragon means an unremitting chain attack aimed at forcing the opponent into total submission. Dragon relies mainly on speed and an unrelenting offensive attack to conquer its enemy.

Dragon style is a sister system to the white eyebrow style. It originated at the same time, and the grandmasters of each system were close friends who had studied kung fu together. Dragon kung fu was founded by the monk Tai Yuk. Tai Yuk's best student was Lam Yiu Kwai, who became the grandmaster of the system, and was responsible for opening it to the Chinese public. The dragon system is a highly-aggressive form of kung fu, relying on speed and pressing the opponent relentlessly until he drops to the ground in defeat. Besides hard external strength, dragon uses a lot of internal power with each strike.

The most important aspect of the system is the *mor kiu* or "arms touching" form. This is taught only after the student has completed two or more years of basic training. The mor kiu form contains the keys to dragon strength and power. These are the same as in white eyebrow kung fu. They are the five external strengths: eyes, mind, hands, waist, and stance; and the five internal strengths; spirit, purpose, endurance, chi, and power (ging).

Power and external strength comes upon impact, and then drives through the opponent. The dragon practitioner must have loose wrists and shoulders. He executes many strikes with his forearms, and spends much time conditioning them. His elbows are always in close to the body, so close that they can't be seen from the back. Keeping the elbows close-in protects his ribs and makes it easier for him to block an oncoming punch. The shoulders are always down and the chest concave, to allow for the expulsion of energy while striking the target. The dragon stylist eventually develops permanently stooped shoulders as a result of keeping his chest concave and his shoulders rounded.

He clenches his teeth tightly when he hits his target. He believes that the force from his blow is expended, not only out his fist, but partially absorbed back through his own body. If he doesn't clench his teeth, this force could break blood vessels and damage nerves to the brain, causing a stroke. So, he tightens the muscles in his neck by clenching his teeth and stops the power from reaching his head.

Dragon footwork is a smooth flowing movement, described as slide-stepping. The knees are turned in for protection and the dragon practitioner will almost glide in a sideways manner towards his opponent. Stances include the bow and arrow stance, side stance, forward stance, and the "goat capturing" stance where 60 percent of the weight is on the front foot. Advancing movement resembles an imaginary dragon, a sideways shuffle with a lot of hip action.

As far as hand techniques go, the dragon stylist relies on a regular fist with which to strike. He doesn't use any specialty fist such as the phoenix fist for which white eyebrow is known. Dragon practitioners will use their forearms and the heel of their palms. The system is famous for its dragon claw open hand strike, which is characteristically a grab, a pull towards him, and a strike with the heel of his palm.

Since the dragon system is taught by only a small number of practitioners in North America, few people have seen it to appreciate its superb blending of both external and internal powers.

Southern Praying Mantis: The "Machine Gun" Striking System

Southern praying mantis kung fu had its origins during the Ming dynasty and was taught only to members of China's royal family. At that time, the system was known as *jew gar* or "royal family" kung fu. With the advent of the cold-blooded Ching dynasty, the Emperor and his family fled to the Northern Shaolin temple to escape certain death at the hands of the Manchurians. But, the forces of the Ching followed, knowing that a revolutionary spirit was being nurtured within the confines of the Shaolin monastery, and burned the Northern temple to the ground. The royal family escaped and moved to the Shaolin temple of Southern China, where, aware that the forces of the Ching were looking for jew gar practitioners, they changed the system's name to Southern praying mantis, hoping to trick the Manchurians into believing that their style was the same as the popular Northern praying mantis. Still, the Manchurians pursued and burned the Southern temple. A number of the royal family escaped death and went into hiding. They became known in Southern China as *hakka* or "Northern guests." From

that time on, the art of southern praying mantis was taught secretly to hakka only, for fear that Manchurian spies would betray them. Even now, in Hong Kong, southern praying mantis is taught only to hakka descendents.

Unlike northern praying mantis, the southern style bears no resemblance to the insect and is strictly a short hand system. Southern praying mantis is quick, direct, and effective. Mantis practitioners do not give their opponents a chance to deliver more than one blow. The practitioner attacks rapidly until his opponent falls down and is disabled. The theory is to get your opponent off-balance and not let him regain it; at the same time, shift in close and attack with many rapid-fire short strikes. The opponent must desperately try to ward off this barrage of machine gun-like blows; but the mantis practitioner won't stop until his attacker is down. Speed is essential. The fist isn't withdrawn to the waist as in karate and some other kung fu systems as the practitioner has to be able to hit many times from the same position. Mantis practitioners don't draw back—it's too slow—and they don't change their basic stance while fighting. That's also too slow. The mantis slides forward and shifts his weight from side to side, backward and forward with each attacking punch. Instinctive reaction is vital due to the speed of the attack. He learns to attack by feel; he knows without thinking what his opponent's next move is and acts quickly to close all avenues of attack.

There are no actual blocks in the system, since the opponent isn't given the opportunity to strike back. The initial block is more of a push to redirect the force of the attacking blow. They don't use force against force in praying mantis; again, that wastes valuable time. They redirect the blow and immediately counterattack.

Power comes from the feet through the legs and up out the fist. The entire body becomes the driving force. Basically a close-in fighting system, southern praying mantis is known for its one-inch punch, similar to the one-inch punch that Bruce Lee used so much.

Many of the strikes are open palm attacks which is a faster strike to deliver. The characteristic fist of the system is the phoenix eye fist, which the mantis practitioner uses to attack pressure points.

Southern praying mantis kicks are all low below the waist, in order to maintain balance and speed. Low kicks are harder to block because the mantis will punch and kick at the same time.

Training equipment includes metal marbles for strengthening the fist, wooden dummies, hanging bags, and wall bags, all designed to improve the mantis' speed, coordination, and balance.

The True Tradition of Kung Fu

There is one thing that all Chinese martial arts have in common: the idea that kung fu itself is merely a skill. Of course, it's a skill that requires serious and diligent training to perfect, but it is still just a skill that anyone can learn. The literal translation of *kung fu* is "a skill or knowledge of something physical." The real value of Chinese martial arts goes beyond self-defense alone. It lies within the strong traditional training that all kung fu systems emphasize: training that teaches the kung fu student to respect his teacher and his teacher's advice; to be respectful toward other kung fu styles, because they are all part of China's legacy; and, perhaps most important, to only use his kung fu skill in a morally correct manner.

UNIQUE LITERARY BOOKS OF THE WORLD

Also Publishers of
INSIDE KUNG-FU and *INSIDE KARATE* magazines